ANIMALS ALL AROUND

by Lindy Norton

© THE MEDICI SOCIETY LTD · LONDON · 1995   Printed in England   ISBN 0 85503 162 X

Aardvark

Albatross

Adder

Armadillo

A

a

Alligator

Ant

Ant-eater

Bullfinch

Bee-eater

Baboon

Blackbird

Butterfly

Bandicoot

B

Bison

Beaver

b

Badger

Bee

Camel

Chaffinch

Chicken

Chameleon

C

Cow

Chinchilla

Cuckoo

Cheetah

Cat

Dove

Dolphin

Dragonfly

Deer

Duck

Donkey

Elephant

Eagle

Elk

E e

Emu

Flycatcher

Flying Squirrel

Falcon

Frog

Flamingo

F f

Fox

Ferret

Guinea Pig

Giraffe

Gerbil

G g

Greenfinch

Grasshopper

Gibbon

Gazelle

Goat

Gorilla

Goose

Gosling

Hare

Hummingbird

Hamster

Hedgehog

Hippopotamus

Heron

Hyena

Horse

h H

Iguana

Ibis

Jerboa

Junglefowl

Ii

Ibex

Jj

Jackal

Kestrel

Kite

Kingfisher

Kangaroo

Koala

Kiwi

Kudu

K k

Lapwing

Lark

Ladybird

Lynx

Leopard

Lemming

Llama

Lizard

Lion

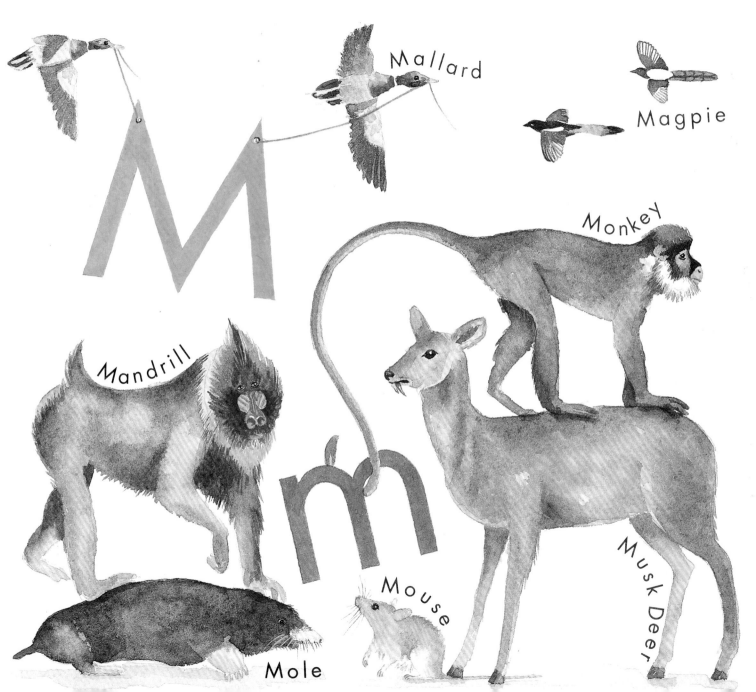

Mallard

Magpie

Monkey

Mandrill

M m

Musk Deer

Mouse

Mole

Nightjar

Nightingale

Narwhal

Newt

Numbat

Owl

Orang-utan

Ostrich

Osprey

Otter

Oryx

Plover

Penguin

P

Parakeet

Parrot

Pelican

Peacock

Pig

Platypus

Puffin

Pipit

Porcupine

p

Panda

Polecat

Qq

Quail

Rabbit

Robin

R

Raccoon

Rhinoceros

Rat

r

Reindeer

Sandpiper

Skylark

Swallow

Skunk

Squirrel

Stork

Shrew

Stoat

Seal

Smooth Snake

Snail

Sheep

Toad

Toucan

Tern

Tit

Treecreeper

Thrush

Tiger

Turkey

t

Turtle

Tortoise

Uakari

Umbrella Bird

Viper

Vulture

Vole

Wren

Weasel

Wolf

Wildebeest

Wallaby

W

Woodpecker

Wagtail

Wasp

Whale

Walrus

X x x

Y y Y

Yellowhammer

Yak

Zebra

Z z Z

Yellowlegs

Zorilla